The Most Charming Creatures

THE
MOST
CHARMING
CREATURES

POEMS

GARY BARWIN

Copyright © Gary Barwin, 2022

Published by ECW Press
665 Gerrard Street East
Toronto, Ontario, Canada m4m 1y2
416-694-3348 / info@ecwpress.com

LIBRARY AND ARCHIVES CANADA CATALOGUING IN PUBLICATION

Title: The most charming creatures : poems / Gary Barwin.

Names: Barwin, Gary, author.

Identifiers: Canadiana (print) 20220184402 | Canadiana (ebook) 20220184429

ISBN 978-1-77041-661-1 (softcover)
ISBN 978-1-77852-026-6 (ePub)
ISBN 978-1-77852-027-3 (PDF)
ISBN 978-1-77852-028-0 (Kindle)

Classification: LCC PS8553.A783 M67 2022 | DDC C811/.54—dc23

Editor for the Press: Michael Holmes / a misFit book
Copy editor: Emily Schultz
Cover image: Gary Barwin
Cover design: Jessica Albert
Author photo: George Qua-Enoo

M I S F I T

The publication of *The Most Charming Creatures* has been generously supported by the Canada Council for the Arts and is funded in part by the Government of Canada. *Nous remercions le Conseil des arts du Canada de son soutien. Ce livre est financé en partie par le gouvernement du Canada.* We acknowledge the support of the Ontario Arts Council (OAC), an agency of the Government of Ontario, which last year funded 1,965 individual artists and 1,152 organizations in 197 communities across Ontario for a total of $51.9 million. We also acknowledge the contribution of the Government of Ontario through the Ontario Book Publishing Tax Credit, and through Ontario Creates for the marketing of this book.

PRINTED AND BOUND IN CANADA   PRINTING: COACH HOUSE   5   4   3   2   1

none of the letters
of plums are in
icebox. only some
of the letters of
forgive me are.

Table of Contents

If I were to cry out
the questions of why or how or
who would hear us—
I'd say the only ones to hear this
are ourselves.
Therefore it is scrupulous to listen.
Especially to the shadows.

— RACHEL BLAU DUPLESSIS,
DRAFT, UNNUMBERED: "PRÉCIS"

DUST
OF
THE
WREN

Dust of the Wren

after William Bronk

we thought she was dust of the wren
but no one has taken the world from us, no
we were watching, yes
dust of the wren, we were watching over

I won't claim
for Alice Burdick

this is all that happens
but I will say it is a true
representation of what you see here.

By the time you finish reading
you will be older. Sadder.
Wiser. If you were a flower and
you read this, you would be a flower
desired by bees.

You lie in the green bristles
friend to grass, lover of grass, ally of softness
and open like petals. That's where
the bee gets in, shimmies through pollen.

I won't claim the calm of sky but
you've got a good view there
on the grass and you think
what you can. Jams. Jellies.

Small faces floating peacefully, closed eyes
like petals. It's your brain
that's a can. Inside things float that last.
Summer song. An old bicycle. Beer.
Your children loving you the length of
their lengthening bones.

You sit to a bowl of clam chowder made by
daughter. A hurricane. Sugar cane.
Citizen Kane. Abel's brother. Day seeps
over one horizon making room
for night to pour over the other

I won't claim night
for dreams where you're double
booked for funerals. Goodnight mother.
Grandpa. Father. Or that life

represents your life. If I had to choose
between bee and flower I'd
choose summer day.

Several Fishes Can Walk on Land

the hip bone is a sacral rib
within the fish we studied
a sacral rider —
hello

several fjords walk on landslides
walk on flashbacks
flame-thrown latch-key
walk languid

the hive bookcase is a rifle
secretly walking lanterns
fistfuls waking landowners
flames milling a lasso

the hoax cooking is a sacral rig
a morphological vehicle
that secretly walks on lapels
a subject consistency

a sacral right-hander that
washes larches
morphological vendettas
secretly wilting lard

the hobo shelf is a sacral rigmarole
a submarine consonant
secretly walloping clerks
flash cubes wait laughs

secret larval welks
a wet-dream larynx
the holograph boozer's sacral ring
a secreted lash

those with the most robust "hip"-bones have
the best walking ability
several fishes warp land

After Edward Thomas's "Adlestrop"

Yes, I woke up
not rebirth but
an agreement with the engine
of the body

I was alone and thought of
translation, took a favourite poem
to Google
Māori, Hawaiian, Zulu, Finnish:

a hedgehog of carcinogens
a June engine.
Now the sun sets
and nothing went wrong

there are tears on the wall.
If you remove the leaves
the sea small but hidden
come closer, closer: we are in pain

the words Oxfordshire and Gloucestershire
didn't translate but still
all around us blackbirds
and a mist of more distant birds

mistier and mistier
the more distant birds.

Thirty Minutes Late
for James Cairns

Reader, I apologize
I apologize
profusely
I am 30 minutes late
for this poem
which is ironic because
for years I have had a recurring
dream about being
30 minutes late
for the beginning
and now
the poem has started
without me

Pact of Oblivion

Hummingbirds see colours the human brain can't imagine
It's hard to describe what blue looks like
even harder to describe when you can't speak

New research suggests the moon is rusting
particularly at the poles
a reddish-black form of iron on its surface

In crickets, the singing species have good hearing
Under a picture of a serious-looking soldier, bayonet drawn:
"Some years ago, we were badly governed

Every day in the streets shots were fired"
Frogs and toads hearing with a membrane
near their eyes

Insects with hearts
and blood but
no lungs

Say something

Everything

I am going to put
          everything
into a poem
but
          in a way
          that appears
invisible

Limerick
for Stuart Ross

A wonderful sadness is the pelican.
Day's shimmer holds more than his belican.
He can take in his bearskin
Enough foothold for a weird
But damned if I see how rhyme helps.

Entirely

hats rise
or
hats set
the horizon
fills with them

they're here
to order sandwiches
reconcile accounts
maybe smoke
listen to jazz

I think of the creases
in pants
of how
hats walk past
so much

how day and night
like hats
surround
your head
entirely

Gargantuan Orangutans
for A. G. Pasquella

philosophy, hot pants, Hot Pockets and orangutans
what if everything ended in orangutans
the way it sometimes ends in orgasms and the one percent
society folded like fleshy origami into monstrous orangutans
Frankensteinian orangutans, gargantuan orangutans
post-industrial enlightenment orangutans our skin
tanning orange in an organum of light
an orange sun making orangutans out of all of us
while long-fingered we squat glumly peeling oranges
the shooting range of modernity kapow kapow kapowing
the foreign tang of bullets above our shaggy made-orangutan heads
and we with doleful earnestness arrange oracles out of rind
fallen on the orangutan-coloured sand of Indonesian shores
what does it say? the future like a newfangled orangutan gets
entangled with our idea of the future and we all pile into an electric
black sedan for a test run of our regret
all of us orangutans looking for the gluten-free
pangs of what could have been a new age, a triumph for orangutan
compassion, income distribution, and the end of everyone going ape
who has the privilege and ability to go ape
and somewhere down the highway our cell goes off
and we know like the world and these words
it's all just clang clamour and meaningless harangue
and it's the orangutan lover of us saying
"you rang you handsome man?"
but it's the end and we still have unused rhymes
Van the Man, Iran and Afghanistan among them

Claims

we're polemical
pour out

back hair
Lauren Bacall
cleats

shrimp boats
attention
bacteria

from open mouths
soon we reach

land that:
1. sparkles
2. thanks us
3. knows what to do
4. you call those mountains?

Disguise

one boy wears
the face of another
the other wears
the first boy's face
like a swim

*

two dogs run a race
the dogs imaginary
the race real

or the inverse:
no one outside the dog

*

at the vowel museum
a long hall fenced with teeth

"I . . . ," begins Martin the cleaner
leaning on his mop

Noon

everything is not
one lemon at a time
various blimp machines
a smoke alarm and cars
Yogi or yogurt
a wounded owl held close
several boxers on a fire escape
a harpsichord

I Have No Words

I'm not going to speak
No I will take no air
from those who should speak
from those to whom we should listen

I'll not take space
but step
aside though you see
in talking about

leaving the stage
and not speaking
about not speaking about
not speaking
it's not my time so

here I am
still speaking about
not speaking
about not speaking

and here I am
oh yes it's not
those who would not speak
should not speak

even about not speaking
see here the pretty
words lined up along
the end of this poem

the poem ending with
the words
my own words

Alas

alas, who was the third one weeping?
I thought we were only two!

— HOSSEIN PANAHI

who was the fourth one weeping?
I thought we were only three

who was the fifth one weeping?
I thought we were only four

who was the sixth?
I thought we were only

the seventh?
the eighth?
I thought we

n weeping + 1
our understanding n - 1

substitute for weeping
writing with one hand
scratching behind a dog's ear with another

a thousand news streams I'm not
watching
substitute for I

blue heron lifting from pond
behind Walmart
Walmart lifting off becoming comet

and we wait
10,000 years
for its return

Goodbye

Goodbye lungs, surly twins, little trees. Goodbye dark. Goodbye
tarmac path. Goodbye each breath, each step. Goodbye buildings,
waving people, elevators and our super, puffing ciggies while
mopping floors. Goodbye he nods but what about the koalas?
We had eucalyptus but now we have fire. Goodbye eucalyptus,
goodbye twins with fire and money. Goodbye fire and money, twins
and habitat. Goodbye city of Hamilton, Ontario. We walk into
the dark, take habitat with us. Goodbye shins against the flames,
fingers tangled with sky. Goodbye mouth a river, eyes two islands
lost in flood, cars underwater but who can tell? Goodbye speech
and sight. Goodbye streets and mortgages, ravines and furrows,
furloughs, tongues and mathematics. Goodbye clouds, streetcars
filled with fish or birds, our hands gripping oceans. We are leaving
now. We are leaving because tangled in this net the ocean comes
with us.

How to End a Poem
for Terese Mason Pierre

you're a corpse

or milk

burnt words
delivered in an envelope
to the mother of your enemy

the mother of your enemy
is a mirror

you're the mirror

a poem is a chair
in a room that has a chair
the poem is tied to the chair

you're the corpse
or the milk
that has found its way inside

the poem

light doesn't stay with milk
what does this mean?

to have a choice
don't begin

don't stop

Barring Withness

land of the

not land of the

home of the

not home of

everywhere

surrounded by

surrounded by

withoutness

Phases


```
  m m
m o o n
m o o n
  n n


  m m
m o   n
m o o n
  n n


  m m
m o   n
m o   n
  n n


  m m
m     n
m o   n
  n n


  m m
m     n
m     n
  n n
```

Errata

p 8 lan- guage
p 9 Crea- tures
transpar- ent
p 11 hap- pen
16 space- time (seems ok?)
17 episte- mological
non- squirrel
19 Listen- ing
num- ber
23 dear- est
his- tory
invisi- ble
them- selves
31 ris- ing
mem- ory
lit- tle
Snow- fall.
bliz- zard,
disap- pear,
gen- erous
35 return- ing
39 bur- ied?
42 float- ing
round- worm
With- out
bor- ders,
43
invis- ible,

Mountains
for Stevie Howell

What do you expect of a poem?
My daughter, aged six, draws
a map of our house and fills the rooms with
giant dogs. The first is called Mountain. The second
is called Mountain, too. The third dog, big as a bedroom,
is also Mountain. Really? I ask. No, she says.

E & O
for Alessandro Porco

I.

let's say
night is a famous singer
and day is love

or the guy with the lyre is time
followed by space
in this case, hell

why can't he just walk
not look back
it's creepy leading and stalking

leave me safe here
eyeless deathless
timeless dark

but Orfeo the yard
and Euridice the beautiful
lawnmower sky

or Euridice a hotdog
and Orfeo a talented
condiment

everything means
two humans separated
dividing here & now

metaphysics means
never having to say
things change

2.

cow
lawnmower
sky

moon
baseball
dog

sorrow
a name for a small sad
bird

did the mention
of hotdog up there
spoil the mood?

an empty song
an open mouth
the throat always filled with shadow

3.

if time is Sisyphus
I'm the rock
happy

in unconstellated sky
refusing to play either
Euridice or

her Orfeo
now I'd like to make the joke about
Oreo

but you know
bathos and bathtub
like twilight refuse

clocks
dark light dark
light dark light

dark light light dark
another meme:
Charon like Cerberus

has three heads
be like Charon & dog
wear many hats

4.

I apologize
the poem has
come to this

but subject and object
light and shadow
burger and bun

song
singer
sung about

listener
reader
writer about

death-convincing
regret-inducing
free-will-problematizing

love
and love
and love

this is where we are

Thank you

We are unable to accept
these poems

We are on fire and possibly
infected. The Poetry Editorial Board responded

strongly, admiring your craft and total rage
but disagreed about how to extinguish

fire or end infection.
Eat the rich.

They're not infected. The poems struck
like bowling balls in a flu

knocking readers down.
We coughed. Our flesh burned. Yet

our eyes are the same old eyes.
Other readers may respond

differently if they're in quarantine
or underwater.

Maybe in time
the poems will find good homes

far from shrieking coastlines.
We hear the shrink of birds

forests denuding foxes. Our offices have returned
to nature. Moss grows on our managing

editor. Our tweed unravels
an economy of entropy.

Like trees our inbox
warps time.

And like time, our out boxes
are on fire and like your blood

you should certainly keep
these poems in circulation.

This is the way the world ends
Not with a bang but
while we watch.

How to Draw a Face

On the slopes of nose, villages like eyes
Eyeholes where eyes are
Guidelines for where to cry

Open mouths wet as wells
Ears where we use them

Hair like wind because the wind, too, ripples
Top of head touching sky

Three

who put the panic
into this little poem?
glad it ends so soon

*

how small
can
                    I make

      this poem

too late

*

let's turn the paren-
theses inside out so that
we mean everything

For/after Hugh Thomas

life is long
life is long
(don't worry)

except for its sudden end
(I mean it)
here we say something about love

life is long
foot falls
the war

but like I said
I said
except for its end

life is long
(don't worry)
(don't)

a sudden end means
it was a rocket
a rocket

like a foot fall
a foot fall
landing on the ground

like maybe when you were running
running
until the end

but of course I miss you
I miss you
you're not here

not here
and all I can do
is walk

Coffee and Triumph

The customers with bicycles or dogs outside
wait for coffees
White or black or brown, hot or cold

My poodle grew up with a girl
He loved her as they walked
Sniffing the path

He has a great stay
And even greater eyes
In this regard
he is my king, my elder

You are leaving
with him
And there you go

Sad Poem

It's really great and so, so sad.
It's not me, it's not the woman or the dog.
It's not the coffee. It's neoliberalism.
Does it construct the greatness of the poem or its sadness?

We're inside it. How could we tell?
What an even sadder story:
the sad poem is stuck inside
a sad poem and does not know itself.

Sandwich

bread
something else
bread

bread
something else
something else
bread

bread
something else
something else
something else
bread

bread
something else
bread
something else
bread

something else
bread

something else

bread
bread

After "What We Are," by William Bronk

Let's say we want to be true.
What is the purpose?
We know things here and there,
supposedly.
Language is worth it,
dangerous bait.
We say we are, we say we are one
We say we should be the same
but oh, no. No.

THE
SWEET
ESPECIAL

Morethan

after Charles North

darker than light you are
lighter than invisible

invisibler than a wall you are
wallier than ocean

you are more oceanic than toast
toastier than snow

snowier than soup you are
soupier than tectonic plates

you are tectonic platier than a rose
rosier than nothing

After "Gute Nacht" from Winterreisse by Wilhelm Müller
English translation by William Mann

A stranger I arrived here
a stranger I leave
Time was good to me
clocks were flowers
Some spoke of love

Two o'clock is my mother
Three o'clock is my mother
Four o'clock is my mother
By five o'clock I am my own father
and my children look like arrows

Now the world is dismal,
the path veiled in snow

I am on a journey
stop at the gas station, buy a Twix
gas up

I must pick the way alone
through this darkness
must choose the correct size
of coffee with sweetener

The mooncast shadow of my SUV
my companion
and on the grey meadow of the sideroad
I look for deer's footprints

Let stray dogs howl
outside the movies
Let students play beer pong
in illuminated front windows
Let signs say, SPEED HUMP
LIFT PLOW BLADE HERE

Love loves to rove
the road waits patiently
ready to be made into metaphor
the deer run into it
unaware

You probably cannot hear my footsteps
as I step on the gas
as I step on the brake

I am a deer in the headlights of deer
eventually reach over
open the door to the deer
then soft, softly shut the door

As I leave I write
"Goodnight" upon the roadside snow
so that, Dear Reader,
you see I have been thinking of you

Names of the Hare

after Seamus Heaney's translation from the Middle English

a man met his left leg
all is not right

a man met his right leg
all is still not right

unless he descend from the ground
what he holds in his hands
what he blesses with arms
how he forgets peace

but let's interrupt
our story to speak the names of rabbits

scum-from-shed, pus-gravel
beat-the-child, donkey-pot

weight-loser, narrow-arrow
home-late, sky-daddy

wife-of-hate, blue-eyes
eyes-of-wall, hedge-hidden

stayabed, coupon-colour
fakebreath, twitterbark

race-monkey, unusual-ear
double-pill, air-pollution

turbo-nose, Olympic-bid
blood-hashtag, Herb Alpert

I look forward to you
shake-in-heart, lambs-are-flying

gum-sucker, awesome-Pete
make-believe salmon-snack

man who cares for the fear of all
one who is afraid to call it

all this happened
and you can go a long way
to the east
to the west
to the south to the north
wherever you are willing to go

and now, man meeting his right leg
and his left upon the green
a wonderful day to you
I come to my dead family
like legs

Weather Report

she at the bottom of a well
with an emperor
the trains travel to thirsty cities

why do they not travel to the well?
why do they not rescue her?
is it the emperor

his bad breath
inconceivable power
his eyes burnt to coal?

he weeps and she feeds him worms
he weeps and she cuts him
he weeps and she plunges her head into the wound

she wears the emperor like a hat
little emperor legs, little emperor arms
skittering in air

she at the bottom of a well
wearing the emperor like a hat
drinks his tears

The Sweet Especial

after "Binsey Poplars" by Gerard Manley Hopkins

Yeah world air cage for aspens dear
sun leaping sun
quelled or quenched
then leaping sun again
                    not spared, not one
                    shadows that swam or sank
meadow & river &
                            mind-wandering weed-minding bank
we yadda and blah but
        listen
"if we but knew what we do
        [though we do]
when we delve or hew —
                    the growing green
            since country is so tender"
[an interruption for]
        the temperature rises
if poetry is impossible after
then perhaps before —
this blue and seeing ball
soon no eye at all
a warning, courage, collectivity
strokes of havoc unselve
rural urban scene, urban rural scene
apostrocene & possessive
and after-comers cannot guess the beauty been

CanLit Fires

with binoculars I could see
My Best Stories by Alice Munro
naked in the lake
with an Introduction by Margaret Atwood
just beyond the island

we'd made love for days
My Best Stories by Alice Munro and me
with an Introduction by Margaret Atwood
it was short fiction
but it was sweet

My Best Stories by Alice Munro
in a kayak
with an Introduction by Margaret Atwood
or in a canoe
the pine shoreline & its reflection a soundwave

and *My Best Stories* by Alice Munro
across the lake
a shooting star across the dark cottage sky
and the night before I'd fallen face forward into the fire
with an Introduction by Margaret Atwood
a shooting star clutching another artisanal beer

oh love was made, it rampiked like lightning
My Best Stories by Alice Munro all week thundered
how would I lie to those I loved
with an Introduction by Margaret Atwood
how would I explain my love, this loss

my little heart singing the shape of the lake
and the ripples there because of the wind
and inside golden light and chainsaws
and Crokinole and I stood under the stars the edges
of me no different than the dark dark cottage sky

John Clare Ghazal

mingle did her hair with her hair and clothes
although herons alight on the beach

it's good to jump on the scales of justice
in the highest half of the tree

next to his body he made his bed
wood cuts the light

in the place where darkness will be darkened
discuss

in gardens, you garden
25 trucks running

protect the soil with soil
now use these small branches and start again

The Softiad

Citizens! let us celebrate our heads
throw our hats in the air

the night is soft
and inside our heads

it is soft as night
a comet passes between father and mother

it is soft between father and mother
inside the baby it is soft also

inside heroes it is soft
everything is so soft that
hereafter we worry not

Haiku

five snowcapped mountains
seven snowcapped mountains, ah
five snowcapped mountains

Skylark

let's say a skybird's scarred ribs
bone-house bell sure bonged a tree-sized bird
yeah a bird-sized um bonsai labouring in hello the ditch between
teef and a turf of shout

a deadly thanks droop cells
okay burst barriers dust preggers then yeah rage
so haha know wot I mean sweet-fowl dunno
song-fowl hey — the grey goose braves another eureka

then we rest yadda yadda cheers from the hearing and babble
drop down the nest
but our own, sure, wild and understood
braided with prison wow shut-eye

jeez the flesh-bound are best when found say beside cukes
meadow fowl, morning trees, well the meadow downy with dew
distressing the rainbow bones holy hello cow
the feet too have so many bones wow imagine clouds

Thrill Ride

Someone was pregnant.
It was my mother.
Hurray! I am to be born.

Then I was.
"You have to be this tall to ride," they said.
"Didn't think you'd be so small."

Then they went away
to look at a lifesize hologram of a whale.
It breached and leapt at the ceiling.

It looked like there was an actual whale in the room
and someone was
whipping the floor with a river.

The Ship of Theseus

what is everything in the world
close by me
my fingers
envelopes
Malarky by Anakana Schofield
a stapler
dog
phone call
elastic band
passport
Seven Classic Albums of Eric Dolphy
cheque to me
change of address
to do list
cheque to my son
shoehorn
old phone
the widow
driveway
shrubs
car
gazelle
recycling box
flat land
the Escarpment
school
new planets which may possibly sustain recognizable life
Wellington boots from when I was six
from p. 6: would a bit of distraction help
Telemann: Complete Suites and Concertos for Recorder
thought about Adam naming things, forgetting verbs

thought from Maggie Nelson quoting Wittgenstein
        about the inexpressible in the expressible
this sense of the year as if it were a thing
remembered conversation
AKAI professional APC Ableton controller
brass letter opener in the shape of an old knight, possibly Don
    Quixote

Spoons
after Lucretius 2.1–9

Sweet it is, when forks are troubling the waters,
to look, from the vantage point of a spoon, on the distress of another

not that the sight of another's fork is in itself a delightful pleasure
but rather because it is sweet to see what forks you are without

Sweet, too, to look upon the massive struggles caused by forks
arrayed on the sides of plates, when you have no stake in the meal

But nothing gives more satisfaction than to dwell in a spoon
a convex moon in night broth

From there you receive signals
messages from the obvious, comb-filtered by forks

you, curled fetal in its silver funhouse
one enormous eye fixed on truth

Brainsnail
after Lucretius 1.936–943

just as eyebrows by the brain are raised
we touch the rim around the world
with the sweet, golden liquor of thought
it tricks us
and works as far as the lips
so that meanwhile we drink down the raw
world's juice
the intent is deceptive not malevolent
and we try to lift trees like eyebrows
squeeze history's tectonics with our mind
make things with an *I Dream of Jeannie* nod
this possessive, this past, this gerund, this goat
this cow, echidna, ghost, carfentanil
pancakes, poems, dusklight
who is this "we" we make drink the world?
not birds but wingspeed
what Francis Ponge writes:
words. decency. our humanism

Rain

after Lucretius 3.830–842

Death is nothing to us, and matters not a road
since the soul is held to be like rain

Just as in times past we had no sensation and were not troubled
when we were the rain coming from all sides around the family car

and we on impact shook hard with tumult
trembled and quivered around Dad's jokes and Mother's breezy
    compromises

and no one knew which of us would win empire
and rule over family

just so, when we no longer are, when brother is gone from family
— those parts whose whole is our being —

nothing can happen, be sure of it, nothing can happen to us then
for then we shall not be, and nothing can make us feel

not if brother dissolves into rain, and from rain to puddle
and puddle to small rivulets which stream into the drain and darkness

But then this water, here where I kayak
here in this river, this lake

here under this flock of wintering & unmovable geese
here on its way to the rising salt sea

Something Else

it's been raining all night
and I can't sleep
half-remembering a poem

Dave McFadden, you said
we should write every day
and today was your funeral

your urn was
exactly as you'd wanted:
a Dilbert cookie jar

you wrote
that perfect poem I can't quite remember:
why do we worry?

I don't remember the rest, something like
we're something
and then something else after that

Autobiography of the Other

7 translations of "Tub" from Don Mee Choi's translation of
Kim Hyesoon's Autobiography of Death

1. Store

Attach your head to the box.

Do not shout or write, that's not the problem.

Ghosts, breath, nose, brows, knee
big hands
your time has not yet come.

2. Coo

Light on your room over the ice.

Do not worry, the year after anguish.

Encouraged by the team, the mosquitoes, the controversies,
the pilots involved
birdsong
but your sound did not arrive.

3. Cleaning

Look at your appearance.

Art is your committee for recovery.

Discharged food, fat, batteries, socks, tongue
damage
available always.

4. Day

Sit on the tree.

No wailing, no comment, no worries.

The egg, the nose, the cup, the cream and the head
great
but your time will come.

5. Morning

Cut your head off with your hand controlled by your own head.

Your toes soaked by your own blood.

Your blood, your fur, your breathing, the last beating of your own heart,
huge hands the size of a stopped heart.
Arrive on time for your birth.

6. Night

It's morning morning under your head, under your head.

The new in your blood.

Your blood, milk, sweetness is the result of your heart.
Please tell us how to release you.
Make time for your birth.

7. In the morning

Grapes are mixed with your blood.

I have refreshed your heart.
A strong arm is great in your heart.

Imagine ease.

TV Is Full

I have forgotten how to breathe
rain/forest/disco
no, that's not right: this poem translated from
English to Zulu to Chinese then back to English

the road was dismantled yet continued
I have forgotten how to breathe
are you worried about the storm?
what about corduroy?

birch/stone/skin
animals, hunters
eyes drunk like autumn
the smell of blood

ashes/solstice/burial light
I have forgotten how to breathe
arrested at the eel station wearing corduroy
[is that accurate?]

beach/bath/Longfellow/transistor
the TV is full
go to Jupiter
I have forgotten how to breathe

Higher States

In the art gallery, the wifi password is thegroupofseven7
There's a sign that says 98 Avondale Road, Avondale $434,900
    Call Wanda 792-8331
Last night my father said, it's been a good life.

Question: knowing that we are born with 270 bones but have
206 bones by adulthood since some bones fuse, when I lay on the
toboggan, did I:

1. Look at the sky and wonder about giving SSRIs to dads

2. Slide through the winter air as if my soul were a sleek
   Lawren Harris

3. Break two bones, rendering my new bone total 208, or

4. Recall how I swam in the river when the sun was hot and
   imagined Wanda, Wanda who
   could sell me the Avondale House where I used to
   live and we could be so happy we
   would cook together, walk our dogs, sit by the
   fireplaces, both upstairs and down,
   read together, and go to the internet to share our
   happiness

My father took the veterinary drugs for the dog but didn't die,
though his herpes was cured.

I called 792-8331 and no one answered but just in case I walked down to 99 Avondale and looked over the fence. There were people in the kitchen and so I went over and asked for Wanda. Here, I said, I have $34. I know it's not much. Soon I'll have the other $434,866. Each of us is a wave or a packet of data sent through the air. Some of us sink like the sun and some glide down smooth. I lay down on the sled and waited for the snow to cover me as if I were the land in a famous painting and someone wonderful was using the brush.

Creation
after Thomas A. Clark

I wanted to be a god
great idea!

no
nothing else

blue
dark blue
black

Five Translations about Death
after Bill Knott

1.
when I was young
this is my sentence

2.
I breathe
a babyful of air
connect to all other babies

3.
open your mouth
wanderer

4.
yes, hello —
your power
mysterious in the middle of waving

Baby

I am the midwife of clouds
stratocumulus, cirrus, nimbus

that's nonsense of course
I'm just a baby

invented for this poem
everyone hand out cigars!

my bones, thin as cobwebs
my skin, light as spiders

my bones, light as spiders
my skin, thin as cobwebs

push the midwife says
push

Magic

I get scissors and
cut around the country
then with one pull, a magician whipping
the tablecloth from under the china
I leave the ground naked
I leave the trees, animals,
rivers, lakes, all water
mountains, insects, plants
fields, forests, meadows, grass
canyons, deserts, snow, libraries
everything else is gone
we start again

Thinking Birds

oh sure I'm a tree
without eyelids

a river
all onomatopoeia

kazang!
philosophy

hey what would it be like if the stars
were eyes

and everywhere was looking
you said

and I said
it already is and

yeah I need
help with dread

onion rings?
onion rings

*

so let's talk about bears:
they are big and often brown

like trees?
yes but "sticky" on the inside only

now imagine
if I were a bird who only plucked

those birds
who didn't pluck themselves

and I plucked myself then
hope both exists and does not

conclusion:
an onion ring begins and ends with itself

Sheer Plod

alrighty yes a beginning this morning a kingdom
daylight — *errr* — a pink republic of dawn hey you up
ring wimpling my ecstasy of wing
then off forth on swingtime data too late for baroque
one is ice a skate's heel swept smooth
o the hurl rebuff gliding Tamagotchi
lutz my heart hiding a bird
coffee stirred the achieve the mastery
murmuration of Ding an sich yeah night-o

buckle up brute beauty oh valour and act
plod plume the fire that breaks billions
ahem Times New Roman it lovelier
yeah dangerous O comic sans wonder
sheer pride in blue though
uhh *Silmarillion* embers shine gash-gold
this autumn of our wow overthrown chevalier
cellar spine of leaves swirl and no doubt
heart spurned bleak vermilion yeah
raise horizon a thousand fists to understand um a day

Armadillo Sandwich

an armadillo in darkness
is an armadillo in darkness
or maybe not an armadillo
but darkness in the form of armadillo

news report:
armadillo found in space
armadillo translation:
maybe it's darkness

darkness then darkness then armadillo
darkness then darkness then armadillo
darkness then darkness then armadillo
armadillo

Loss
for Jeremy Hight

I had a big toe
now my big toe is gone

suitcase, sunglasses, Hawaiian shirt
my big toe is gone

travelling
I ask my remaining big toe

where
where has our big toe gone

my remaining big toe says
don't know says

but I'm with you
I'm with you

THE
LAND
OF
HEALTH

Birds

Each day, the philosopher took a walk at precisely one o'clock. It was such a precise routine that they would set the church clock by him. How can you be so precise? they asked the philosopher. I wait until I hear the church clock chiming one, he said.

Joy and Sorrow

Joy, Sorrow and Ape were siblings. They argued about everything. Since they were always fighting, they asked their mom to help.

She tried all sort of things, but nothing stopped the kerfuffle. So, she locked them in their room. "This way they will have to work it out," their mom said.

Many things changed over the years. The alignment of continents. The acidity of the oceans. The climate. Ape evolved into an early form of human but Joy and Sorrow remained the same.

Moral: Joy and sorrow remain the same.

Whale

Whale was balding. He was embarrassed around the other whales so he hung out on the surface of the ocean, spouting sadly. Bird saw that Whale was sad and so he flew between Sun and Whale and covered Whale's bald spot with his shadow. Whale had never been so happy. Then Military Airplane flew into Bird and Bird was turned into feathers. Later, Military Airplane bombed a town but Whale never found out and so he remained happy until the end of days.

Moral: Wear a hat and support journalists.

Barman

Capitalism, Martin Luther and an amoeba walk into a bear. Martin
Luther says, Lord Almighty, I need a nail, I've 95 things to say about
religion. Capitalism says, give a man a nail and he can nail things for
one day, but convince him he's a nail and you can hammer him for
his whole life. Time to split, the amoeba says. Okay, but when do I
get to speak? the barman asks.

Phone Call from John
for John Kameel Farah

This is Glenn Gould. This is Major Tom. This is Frank Shankenheim. This is only the beginning of the end of the beginning. This is a Raid can filled with a deadly harpsichord. This is the 11/10 grass of the front lawn. This is the flat-second in the scale of the rest of your life. This is Goody Three-shoes. This is the bird of not quite so happy as some other birds, but still making it through. This is the bird of Brampton paradise, a bird with many generous and empty parking lots. This is the Manheim crescendo. This is Hanover on a Saturday night sometime in the 18th century and there's a guy in a wig singing a very singable melody in a place that will one day be a Taco Bell. This is knitting seven galaxies into a scarf the size of seven galaxies. This is a border like a fishing line. This is what freedom looks like. This is how we do the moonwalk. This is how you dance like an Egyptian or an Israeli soldier. This is a Rubik's Cube shaped like Palestine, one side all olive trees, the other always-changing sides, safety and an uncle's poetry. This is Terry Riley with safety goggles playing a keyboard made of Etruscan goats in a tuning known only by the goats. And one sheep. This is a joke about a VCR in a suburban basement in the 1980s. Didn't know there was a video of Schoenberg hosting *Saturday Night Live*. This is the old joke about the Apartheid piano where the white keys are separated from the black ones. Where are the brown keys? If I could be any cereal I'd be Franken Berry—no, Kaptain Kaballah, no this is improvised. This is ancient history. This is how we somehow keep moving with a curiosity for the strange, compassionate and beautiful. Now draw this.

Tiny Wings

There's a store in town where you buy grief. We walk in and
suddenly we hear the heartbeats of squirrels from everywhere
in the world. Hedges, lawns, parks, trees, attics, temples, islands,
grottos, oubliettes and ditches. An indistinct roar we feel rather
than hear. Maybe we'll die of that roar. And the grass. It is growing
everywhere, sometimes to seed. The wind roars through the blades
as the blades rise and the seeds begin their thin journey on the
wind. We stumble or march down the shelf-lined aisles, feeling
small or else too large. There are windows. An outside is visible
through their smudged glass. A calendar behind the counter shows
a dream girl resting against an old car. She's old now.

"Our mother," we say, "she asked for grief."

Tiny wings flutter on the back of the teenage clerk, like the
wings of a fly. Tiny wings move on our backs, too. They move
quickly, a small blur, but do not lift us from the ground.

OH
GODDAMN
UNDERSTANDING

Blue Train

So many accordions on the roof of the blue train.
What is history?
The tracks travel to the horizon.
Quick! Let's travel faster than memory.
Now a song.
"So many accordions on the roof of the blue train.
What is history?
The tracks travel to the horizon.
Quick! Let's travel faster than memory."

Saying Chaos like Cows

1.

three cows
two shadows

in a field
the field casts no shadow

as a child, the cow was a calf
the moon was earth

a cow moves

its shadow does not move but
comes into being

three cows
two shadows

the third cow's shadow falls
over the second

how tender is
this absence of light

2.

there is chaos in the field but
I used to play chess with my grandfather

memory is a series of moves
which define the board

water casts shadows
into water below

the shadow of the wind is sound
for example, the trees

in what way is language shadow
how tender is repetition

how tender are
shadows

3.

and cows
the moon is a reflection

the absence of shadow
darkness drains from

three cows in a field
large as a field or chess set

my grandfather gone 25 years
his memories gone like shadow

what can a poem do?
it can refer to itself

4.

again
let's talk to chaos

and cow shadows
tender world-changing

songs
light is chaos with a wet nose

take that!
power structures and night

say something
it means nothing

say something
then say it again

Bombardier Beetles Squirt Boiling Anal Chemicals to Make Frogs Vomit

everyone's a critic and
beauty's a weed in the flowerbox of quiddity
an anthropomorphized blackbird might say
I'm mostly interested in
iridescence and blackbird behaviour
— other blackbird behaviour —
we wear our own shadow
and drive around in fast cars
as for those beetles squirting boiling
anal chemicals to make frogs puke, well
there was one spring morning when it seemed
we were happy

Beard

there was a civilization inside
a giant beard
its people were not walruses
but they were Jews

this was years ago on another planet
each Jew was a fern
and walruses did not exist
I saw a news story about a young penguin

that every dusk
would meet an older penguin who had lost
her partner and the younger penguin
would put his flipper around

the older penguin and they'd watch
the lights of
Melbourne, Australia together
consoled and consoling

Bucket List
for/after Ben Niespodziany

you check into a motel in the desert
the motel that is my head
the desert which is the desert
my head which rests on sand

make it glass
I say to the sand
I say to the sun
but nothing changes

except the towels
and the clerk in the lobby
it's Jim, then it's John, then it's Jim again
once Jim was glass, John was glass, too

you get ice
you watch TV
night falls over our heads
you fall asleep in Room 3

Big Sad
for A.H. Reaume

Napoleon reaches inside his shirt for a kayak

Napoleon reaches inside his shirt for a river

Napoleon puts the kayak in the river

someone—Jacob Wren maybe?—said
the difference between depression and a paddle is
the paddle

Sonnet for International Poetry Day

poetry has hands
bananas
how is a tree like a telephone?
things to burn down:

poetry
a barn
all psalteries
whoever they are

let us follow a radio wave into space
brave little wave are you horny?
heart of a whale unguarded
pie cooling in the open air

Archaeology

1:22 p.m. in the future and I'm Frank O'Hara
dug out a peat bog by miners

the afternoon is a great slap
a freshly cut larch with slashes for eyes

my heart is an inverted teardrop
wide open and slightly unnerving

I'm not a friend of yours
much less an ancient pal

but soon I will scream and shout and sing
scar myself with zigzags and chevrons

what kind of authority — possibly malevolent authority
will I project?

look, it's a miracle that we've survived
it's a miracle that we've survived at all

Big

the world is big
very big

a big baby in our arms
arms are in trouble

sky blue

how is it possible a bird flies?
oh baby

flowers grow between our toes
words like dirty rain

there are thousands of words
and the baby lies

feeling safe
beneath each one

What Things Are the Colour of Sweaters
for/after Baṇuta Rubess

what I bought today

a hammer
a sweater
a dog haircut

one way to end things is to stop talking
I'm writing this and
thinking of what my friend Alex Porco might think

we mistook the sound of a truck
for wind in the trees
the sky the colour of a sweater

fifty years ago
I was a quarter the age of my middle son though
I don't think it means anything

Count the Disco Balls

caution, hot!
there are plants
and rocks
and speakers
here we are
invisible
what's inside us?
cool sex
great distances
folk songs
husks
Liz Howard said on Twitter
that consciousness was
the first and best lie
other than love
though she didn't say
that last part
is love a lie?
there's no way to tell because
this is writing
(on my desk a tube that says
"moisturizing lotion
dermatologist approved")
but my money's on love
which is to say
here

On a Ladder, Looking Up

through the ladder
I see
not the ladder

but a man on a ladder
lassoing a ladder
like a ladder

Portal

1.

look at these words
[ah there's hhhhh fish in my pants it's an old routine ppppppp]

the water is a school of fists
~ ~ ~ ~ ~ ~ ~ ~
ah you can go through whatever
you want to go through 'cause

[footstep footstep footstep]
L   R   L

it's all a portal even
the destination

an eyeful
of fists

door in
the shape of
body
perception
ladders
bassoon solo poorly played

2.

the hands of the children born
day and night
wrapped in cloth

white or black, black or yellow
things in the sea

pigs
pork flowers
cucumbers in a dark bowl
enough to fight

fists in the evening a quiet thought
flowers crablike
but some are happy too

the end of the year remembered
and so on until death

he was buried heartless
the bones joined together
nest, embryo, knot

3.

my children f f f
in metal holes
or one hole

jjjjjjjjj

around the sea
it is very soft

full moon/small moon
evening has a broken mind

the road another handshake
night L   R   L

4.

born in the evening
flowers like flowers

mourning
left R left

the eyelids nest
[breath]
sea is not possible

m m m
the thumb's fruit
O an oboe
a portal where
finally

Commencement for Cootes Paradise

I.

Fish hovering above silt. Their mouths open, hoovering the almost dark.

10,000 Olympic-sized swimming pools. If humans are 60 percent water — heart 73 percent, lungs 83 percent — how many humans is that? Varicoloured humans reaching forward, displacing the river, swimming, floating in liquid sky.

Someone left a valve open.

They told us in science class: Love + Time = Death.

No, wait, my grade nine girlfriend said that. Our world is sensation and memory, our 73 percent brains, our 31 percent bones.

Stellar nucleosynthesis resulting in the complex organic molecules necessary for life formed in the protoplanetary disk of dust grains surrounding the Sun before the formation of the Earth + energy = city counsellors.

24 billion gallons of sewage is what is going on inside of us, while 24 billion gallons of sewage is what we do on the outside. Or, according to David Kessler, grief.

Old David Foster Wallace fish: Morning, boys. How's the water?

Young DFW fish: What the hell is water?"

2.

The moon fills bedrooms, kitchens, basements with its silver, stair-cases slick with shine. Twenty-four billion gallons of fish slide into our homes, our 73 percent brain a stippled perch spawning at night.

Here's the heart pumping under its sheath of shad.

Here's largemouth bass slithering upstream toward heart chambers. A thousand vena cava tributaries, the watershed of our fist-size swims.

A valve releases fish and eels, frogs and water voles into our chests, our "forever" mud rooms and rec rooms. Here fish + eels + frogs + voles = 24 billion gallons of sewage and runoff.

A mouth a kind of valve, open — largemouthed, duckfaced — to the dark everywhere. Here our breathing strained through the weir of our teeth. How many breaths fill an Olympic pool? No. We breathe air, it's the gills of our grade nine girlfriend where water fins.

City counsellors stock pockets with frogs, fish, eels, water voles, lift glasses from their civic desks, tip lakewater in. A sidereal biome. Removeable. A hand's worth of pond or river. Shh, the susurration of rippling. Shh, the secrets held in a closed mouth, a net, a Celtic knot of fish.

What-the-hell water where fish glug and burble, tell-it-truth light slanted toward silt. What is river, is lake, is marsh, is Time + Death = Love.

My grade nine girlfriend and me on the shore of Cootes Paradise, human as driftwood, twig-sized toes sunk and wet in the near shore sandy muck, blood circulating under our high school skin as if across the upper city, combed by waterfalls raked over escarpment cliffs, runnelling down rivers into a lake where our feet stand in the cool and, hands in each other's hands, we open our mouths to the dark, breathe stickleback, tadpole madtom, green sunfish, finescale dace, northern hognose sucker.

How much dark in a river, in a lake or marsh? How much light? Watershed of night, of day. Those with veins. Those without.

No, it wasn't my grade nine girlfriend. And it wasn't me. We weren't looking at 24 billion gallons, its dark surface, 100 billion pounds of starlight gone. A nearly 100 percent full moon.

What + what = this? What + what is here to breathe the silt of this dark night?

Song

I get in a rowboat and row. I'm in the centre of the ocean and around me the fish are like fish but they're also scimitars carving waves from water. Far below, I hear a phone ringing and someone answers it. A vampire squid or a megamouth shark. Piano? a voice says, rising from the deep, wet and braided. I'm the only piano here. Someone wants to talk. There's a song I know. I begin to play it, even the wrong notes. *Dah dah dah dah*, but I've forgotten everything, everything but how quiet it is. And it is so quiet here, too, in the centre of the ocean. The waves like sheep or the hands of a dancer. I close my eyes and Oscar Peterson begins to play. His beautiful long legs, his Little Burgundy heart. A coffin is a piano for a corpse and not song.

Translation from Birds

The sea overrunning its boundaries encounters sweet waters; the wanton flesh assaults the sweet rivulets of tears. By stormy whirlpools the sea obstructs the passage of ships; the stormy flesh plunges the morals of the righteous into the depths. While the sea is disturbed by such great storms, soil is mingled with waves by the crashing of breakers, and thus by the concussion of sea and land the sea receives its mixed colour. Likewise, while the flesh suggests and the soul does not agree, it is as though a certain tone in the body is made from black and white, which tone, made from various elements, is called indecisive. Therefore, the sea colour on the breast of the dove denotes distress in the human mind.

He wants to be better than the enemies of his boxes, who copy false waves; friendship relationships involve theft and crime and technology. Customers want something different from their wild shoes; the things that fall are the righteous who stumble. While these deceptive practices complicate the quest, the solstice influences the weather by combining food and so with sound and noise, the quest finds the best colour. Similarly, where the sample shows and provokes a fight, it is like the skin of a black and white bullet, where the other defenders are called resting. Therefore, the colour of the chest on the clay bricks indicates the separation of exile.

Knowes and Acnotedgements

In 1862 Ernst Haeckel published *Monograph on Radiolarians.* He described radiolarians, ancient single-celled organisms with mineral skeletons, as "the most charming creatures."

The charm quark is the third most massive of all quarks and, along with the strange quark, is part of the second generation of matter.

Look. We're all the most charming creatures. Who? Us. Letters. Words. We neurons.

The title of this book is from a text (which I subsequently edited out of this book) I wrote for an eponymous video work by Catherine Heard. The video was published in the *Heavy Feather Review*, https://heavyfeatherreview.org/2021/05/28/heard-barwin/

Dust of the Wren. Several poems from this collection were published as a chapbook (entitled *Dust of the Wren*) by rob maclennan's above/ground press.

"Several Fishes Can Walk on Land" is adapted from a news article, https://www.nsf.gov/discoveries/disc_summ.jsp?cntn_id=301250

"Hummimgbirds see colours the brain can't imagine" is adapted from an article, https://www.nationalgeographic.com/animals/article/hummingbirds-see-colors-outside-rainbow#:~:text=They%20found%20that%20hummingbirds%20would,of%20plants%20and%20their%20nectar.

"Barring Withness." The left-hand stanza was taken from a sign greasepainted on the window of a van parked somewhere right-wing.

"Thank you" is adapted from a rejection letter from a literary journal. Which one? Rhymes with "Fallow cat."

"for/after Hugh Thomas" appears in the soundtrack for a short film by Derek Jenkins.

Maybe some of these poems appeared in your dreams or your basement freezer, but they also appeared in the following publications (a fact for which I'm very grateful): "Weather Report" in *Spoon River Poetry Review*; "Barman," "The Softiad" and "John Claire Ghazal" in a leaflet by No Press; "Thrill Ride," "Baby," "Thinking Birds" and "Magic" in *Granta Magazine*; "Something Else" in *The Walrus*; "Autobiography of the Other" on the *Burning House Press* blog; "Commencement for Cootes Paradise" in *The Dalhousie Review*; and "Goodbye" in *Watch Your Head: Writers and Artists Respond to the Climate Crisis*, ed. Kathryn Mockler (Coach House Books).

"Bombardier Beetles Squirt Boiling Anal Chemicals to Make Frogs Vomit" is the title of a *National Geographic* video (https://youtu.be/WKEu9oZsh4A).

"Higher States" is for and was written as part of a writing challenge with Ally Fleming.

The first section of "Translation from Birds" is from a translation by Willene B. Clark of Hugh of Fouilloy, *De avibus (The Birds)*.

*

All texts are a lie that reveal a secret about another text. Of course, it's also true that language itself is a lie which reveals a secret, too. But it's always also its own truth. Many of these poems were achieved in part by "translating" a poem by running it many times from one different distantly related language into another using

Google Translate and then finally back to English. Sometimes a process related to N+7 was used, often employing a translator at Spoonbill.org in order to create a beautiful and compelling lie, vivid with secrets.

Some charmed creatures that I'd like to thank sweet especially. Donato Mancini for his invaluable and insightful editorial insights on this book. ("Editing: third time's a charm.") Michael Holmes for sending the manuscript to finishing school with his generous and deft guidance, copyeditor Emily Schultz for gilding the silly with precision and Jessica Albert for the cover and everyone at the mighty charming ECW Press.

Writer friends whose friendship both literary and personal are continuous charms on the entangled bracelet of the writing life: Tom Prime, rob mclennan, Lillian Nećakov, Kathryn Mockler, Stuart Ross, Alice Burdick, Elee Kraljii Gardiner, Franco Cortese, Gregory Betts, Tobias Reber, Catherine Heard, Alex Porco and Derek Beaulieu. Also a happy shout-out to those who read the acknowledgements first. I think it helps one get oriented and get a sense of where the text is coming from, perhaps once the curtain is drawn open. I'm grateful you're here.

Thanks to supporters of public funding of the arts whose beliefs meant that some of this work was written with the aid of grants from the Ontario Arts Council, as well as during writer-in-residencies at McMaster University, Western University, and Laurier Universities, University of Toronto (Scarborough), Sheridan College and the Hamilton and London Public Libraries. The conversations, readings, inspirations and investigations that resulted in some of these poems began there.

Way up there, I spoke about quarks. Quarks are the only elementary particle in the Standard Model of particle physics to experience all four fundamental interactions. Deep gratitude to my wife, Beth Bromberg, who enables me to experience many fundamental interactions, including writing and thus was instrumental in helping create this particular molecule out of the molehill which is language — uhh — life.

The bestselling author of 26 books of fiction and poetry, **Gary Barwin** has won the Stephen Leacock Memorial Medal for Humour, the Canadian Jewish Literary Award, and has been a finalist for the Governor General's Award and the Scotiabank Giller Prize. He lives in Hamilton, ON.